Lord Please Open My Eyes

Daniel W. McMartin

PublishAmerica
Baltimore

First printing

PublishAmerica has allowed this work to remain exactly as the author intended, verbatim, without editorial input.

Hardcover 978-1-4560-4194-6
Softcover 978-1-4560-4193-9
PUBLISHED BY PUBLISHAMERICA, LLLP
www.publishamerica.com
Baltimore

Printed in the United States of America

To the Doak Family ...

No Matter the Storms in life
we must remember God Has a
purpose... But most of all it
is the hardest & darkest of
times when we can experience
his love for us the Most!
we need to simply remember
to open our eyes & look
for him...

[illegible]

Philippians 1:12

Contents

Dedication

To my beautiful wife Sharon and my incredible children: You daily inspire me to be a better husband and dad. Every time I feel that there's no possible way I could ever love you more, you always find a way to prove me wrong.

To Jeff, Grant, Karla, and my Parents: Each one of you has been instrumental in making me the man I am. You have granted me wisdom, creativity, guidance, and love. You have given me gifts that no amount of money could ever purchase, and I am forever grateful.

To Eric, Shawn, Keith, McLean, and Bob: Thank you for being the *True Friends* I needed at the exact time I needed them.

To my Lord and Savior Jesus Christ: Thank you for opening my eyes!

To Clinton: You were the brother that people wish for, but that I was lucky enough to have. Words cannot do justice to the impact you had on my life. Make sure you enjoy heaven until the day I'm blessed to join you.

Introduction

I was alone and completely lost after the death of my brother Clint. That's not to say I had no one around to support me. Quite the contrary, I was surrounded by friends and family who offered an insurmountable level of love and support. Mentally though, I was a complete train wreck. Never before had I lost someone that I loved so deeply, and who had meant so much to me on so many different levels.

To add to my anguish I had become my own worst enemy by holding in all my thoughts and feelings. I thought that I needed to be the "strong one" for everyone else. I found myself trying to protect everyone around me who may have been just as devastated by Clint's death as I was. I didn't want the worries about my mental state to compound the current stresses and burdens that my loved ones were already facing. In essence I would live a lie in order to protect everyone else's feelings and emotional state.

What I found was that by allowing my feelings and emotions to become reclusive, I had become extremely depressed, angry, and confused. I was not the man I once knew, or the one I needed to be for my family and friends. I was in a very dark place, and was blindly leading myself down the wrong path.

The book you hold in your hands is a direct result of God opening my eyes and setting me right again. It's my starting point from that pivotal day in September when things became clear to me. That was the day I felt as if a fire had been lit in my soul, and a weight had been lifted from my heart. Thoughts and emotions poured from my mind and I found an unexplainable desire to record them all. I truly feel the words in this book are "God Breathed", and my hope is that they will help you find the same inspiration and life changing meaning as they have for me.

Make no mistake, the purpose of my thoughts and opinions on these pages are not to invoke some type of theological debate or breakthrough. I don't feel my interpretations of various bible verses should be seen as more profound or poignant than anyone else's. And this most definitely is not a culmination of my rusty translating skills from my senior year of college so as to decipher the ancient Greek text of the Bible. This book simply contains the common thoughts from a common man who was faced with a very uncommon situation. The following word filled pages that lay before you are the end result of that situation. When it boils right down to it, this is my journey before, during, and after the death of my brother.

Though this book leans heavily on dealing with the death of a loved one, my overall intent for writing it is an attempt to help anyone who may have faced, or is currently facing a trial in his or her own life. Since I firmly believe that it is through these trials that we can actually find answers to the question of why God placed these circumstances before us.

I feel this book should be seen as a starting point, or "entry level" if you will, for anyone who may have lost a loved one, is facing a hardship, or has developed a devastating health issue. Whether you do not have a personal relationship with Christ, or have found yourself wavering from the life he wants us to live, my hope is that the words on these following pages may help you find the comfort and answers you have been seeking. There is a message to be found in our trials and our pain if you know where to look. My prayer is that God will use this book to touch your soul and open your eyes so that you too can see the gift in that message.

Psalm 51:9-13

Hey

Hey... Three little letters.... Three silly and insignificant little letters... To most individuals, those three letters make up an ordinary word they hear from time to time. It's a simple and short greeting that's commonly overlooked. But to me, those three letters eco in my mind, and cut to my heart. To me, those three little letters are much more than a simple word or greeting. You see it's those three letters that helped form a bond between my brother and me.

Properly spoken, our greeting was said with a short low blast. One in which you nearly lose the sound of the word's first letter. Dropping your voice and catching only half of the *H*, a person could swear we were actually saying "*ay.*" It is an art form, yet still a simple skill that countless can copy and many could master.

Growing up as the youngest of four boys was often times a rough life to live. Or at least it seemed that way when you were the one who had to live it. Rarely if ever, did I win when we played any number of sports in the front yard. And I honestly can't remember a time when I actually won a wrestling match with any of them. I was picked on, teased, and tormented. Yet luckily, I somehow managed to come out of my childhood having only two small scars, and two broken bones. My right collarbone was broken on two separate occasions, both times at the hands of my brothers. However, if memory serves me, the scars were results of my own accord. Nonetheless, I still maintain that the acts which produced them were in one way or another instigated by my brothers.

By no means do I write this to make my big brothers sound like some type of horrible monsters. They weren't. In fact they were the farthest things from it. We were simply boys, and we played like boys. Sometimes when boys play, things get broken. Since I was the smallest of the bunch, I was typically the one who ended up in tears for some reason or another. Regardless, the life we shared together is a life I would not trade for the world!

Each one of the experiences I lived through helped to make me the man I am today. After all, how many people actually have the chance to watch and idolize three older brothers? I was granted a very rare opportunity in life. One in which allowed me to stand back and learn from the success and failures of three strong men.

Being able to follow in their footsteps has taught me life lessons most people could only wish for. More importantly, even the childhood memories that may have left me with a physical scar, or a small lump on my shoulder; some how today only leave me with a smile on my face.

My sister and all three of my brothers will always have a very special place in my heart. Clint however, has an extremely special place. Not just because we were so close in age, though that does slightly play into it. You see, when the two of us were younger, Clint and I looked very similar in appearance. So similar at times, people would even mistake us as twins.

To me, this was wonderful! There I was, a shy young boy who not only had a big brother I looked up to, but who I also looked like. Teachers at school and friends of the family would often confuse the two of us. Even as late in life as my first year of college I had friends mistake me for him. Clint always maintained that this was slightly annoying for him. Something I would suspect any older sibling could relate to. However, from time to time he would drop hints that despite his outward appearance, he secretly enjoyed it just as much as I.

Time went by, and though Clinton and I always looked like brothers, we slowly began to look less and less like twins. He bulked up, and I kept my skinny track running body. He kept his hair short, I grew mine a bit longer. I grew to 6 feet, and he stopped at 5-11. He could grow a beard by noon, and it took me two days to just get stubble. Regardless of all of our changes as we aged, there was always one constant between us. That constant was that silly little three-letter word.

To hear it slip from either of our mouths would confuse you. We used the same tone, the same influx, and same short half of an *H* technique. I can't begin to count the number of times we confused someone as to which of us two had called them on the phone. Yet somehow, it was much bigger than that.

You see, we never used the word "Hey" sparingly. A person who has spent any amount of time with either of us would know that fact. You may have heard it if you were about to get in trouble, or when we simply wanted to get your attention from across the room. Most commonly however, you heard it as a greeting. This is the way we greeted you when we walked through the door, called you on the phone, or saw you in the hallway.

It's a silly little word. But it's that silly little word that's ingrained in me, and flows from my lips without ever giving it a second thought. Unfortunately, it's now those three little letters that haunt me. Every time I open my mouth and those three letters slip out, I hear my brother's voice, and I miss him a little bit more each time. Clinton was my brother, my mentor, my hunting buddy, and one of my very few "*true friends.*"

The fact he was a *true friend* has always been a bit ironic for me. Since it was Clinton who ingrained in me the meaning behind being a *true friend.* He taught me that any acquaintance could eventually be called "a friend." However, it takes so much more to be someone's *true friend,* and as you age you'll realize what a small percentage of people actually fit that criteria.

Life gets busy, families get started, and people often move away. But the minute one of those select few people walk through the door, something magical happens. It seems as though nothing has ever changed. You're 16 again, and on top of the world! Unfortunately for me, I now have one less *true friend* in my life...

Philippians 4:12-13

Pain

August 13, 2010 was your normal and overly ordinary day for me. Wake up at 4:30 am and get ready for work. I took my normal shower, put on my work clothes, and combed my hair as I do every day of the week. After my normal prep was done, I quietly made my way downstairs, and hopped in my car to make the 22-minute drive to work.

Reaching my destination my normal and repeatable day continued... Enter my office, go through some paperwork, read some e-mails, and prepare to start my employees for a long and hot day's work. My morning continues, and still nothing is out of the ordinary, but then shortly after my lunch break, I receive an email from my mother that would ultimately change my life forever.

To read that email and not know the end results would have very little significance for you. I know this, because it lacked in significance for me the first time I read it as well. My first thought was that it was going to be a typical "checking in with you" note. But this time it wasn't just a simple how are you and the family doing. This note was much more informative than I ever could have realized at the time. Though she did start off with the expected "hope everyone is doing ok," the importance of the email was placed on the very next line. That is where she informed us that Clinton had just gotten back from the doctor, and that they had found a blood clot in his leg. Nothing to get too worked up about though, since it is not near any major veins. However, we are still asked to pray that this remains a minimal and quickly fixed problem for him.

Fast-forward to August 16, and I find yet another email about Clinton in my in-box. This one is written with a little more urgency as it states that Clinton has been suffering from a continuous headache and is sleeping a lot. Once again we are asked to pray for him.

August 17th greets me with two emails. The first telling me that Clinton still does not feel well. He is very fatigued and is tormented by the continuous headaches. Clinton's wife Caryn is very worried, and is once again taking him to the doctor to hopefully see if they can find something new.

The next email reads that the doctors diagnosed him as having a virus similar to mono. They gave him some meds and told him to go home and rest. Unfortunately, the relief I felt after reading that note, was relief I never should have had. It was at that point which I actually began to put my worries out of my mind, and started to go on with my normal every day life.

August 24th 2010 is a day I will never forget. Sitting down in my office for lunch, I open my email and found yet another note from my mother. This one is short, and the tone is filled with urgency and worry. "Dad and Caryn are taking Clinton to the emergency room at Allen Hospital... He has slurred speech and an empty stare. PRAY!!!" I was at a loss, I really didn't know what to think, say, or do. My brother was in trouble, but honestly, deep down, I don't remember being extremely worried. I knew how strong he was. Why would this be anything that he would not be able to beat?

I received numerous phone calls regarding Clint and his progress the remainder of the day and into the night. But unfortunately there was no new ground breaking news offered as the doctors were still running tests.

The next morning my oldest brother Jeff called me at 6:30 am. The minute my cell phone began to vibrate, my stomach sunk and my heart began to race. No one I know ever calls me that early without some type of bad news. Reluctantly, I flipped my phone open and answered to hear Jeff's voice on the other end. Just as my churning stomach expected, the news he has is not good as I listen to him tell me that Clinton was diagnosed with Leukemia. He then goes on to say that they also think he may have had a small stroke, and that they are going to move him to the University Hospital in Iowa City.

Being the big brother though, he still tries to comfort me. He goes on to say that even though this is very serious, Leukemia is a curable disease and that Clinton is a very strong person. I thank him for letting me know, and ask him to keep me updated on any further information. Little did I know that I would only need to wait 12 hours for that information to come.

Standing in the kitchen of my home, the phone rings and my wife Sharon answers. A look of worry flashes on her face, and she hands me the phone. Quickly I grab it from her hands and once again hear Jeff's voice. He tells me that Clinton is not doing so well, and he strongly suggests that I go to the Hospital. Without hesitation, I tell Sharon what I'm doing, and run upstairs to my bedroom. I toss on a pair of jeans, and grab a sweatshirt and hat. Before I even realize what is happening, I find myself making the hour and a half trip from my house to Iowa City.

The entire drive I prayed like I had never prayed before. I pled with God to heal my brother. I begged him to have mercy on his life. As the trip progressed I even found myself talking to Clint. It was almost as if I believed I had some type of telepathic power that allowed me to speak to him. I kept telling him to hold on, and fight for me!

When I finally reached the hospital, I was a complete mess. Time was dragging by, but at the same instant moving so quickly I only remember small chunks of the night. I made my way up to the 5th floor and down the hallway of the ICU. I found my mom, dad, and sister-in-law Caryn huddled in a tiny waiting room barely large enough to fit one more person.

Frantically I asked where he was. Dad spoke up and told me that they had taken him down to get an MRI. They wanted to get a better look at the blood clots that had formed in his body. From that point on, it became a simple waiting game for me. Something I have never been very good with.

Looking at my watch I saw it was 10:00 pm when my oldest brother Jeff and his wife Laurie had finally arrived. I walked down the hall and began to pace. I felt utterly helpless, and it was tearing me apart.

I called Sharon, and told her that there still is no new news, but that I had decided to spend the night there. She told me to call her as soon as I knew anything, regardless of the hour. She too was unable to sleep, and completely filled with worry. I told her I loved her, and would inform her of any new progress. I ended the call and began to make my way back to the micro sized waiting room. As I rounded the corner, a nurse pushing a bed had just exited the elevator. There he was, my big brother...

As I followed them down the hall, I had a feeling come over me that I had not experienced in quite some time. It was the feeling of pride. Not your normal happy for yourself pride. It was the pride that a 10-year-old boy feels as he watches his big brother score the winning touch down of the championship game.

If you have never been a 10-year-old boy with a big brother, this may be a hard feeling to comprehend. The closet thing I can equate to this feeling; is the pride a parent feels for their child during the "first" of anything as they grow.

I distinctly remember walking two steps behind that nurse. Looking down and making out the dark hair of Clint as his head rested on the pillow. I knew he was hurting, I knew he was broken, but as we made our way down that long hallway; all I felt was pride. That's my big brother! And I wanted to tell it to every single person I walked past that night.

The night progressed and not much new news came. The doctor's laid out their plan, and tried to answer questions as best they could. Despite hearing their well laid out plan, I still could not find ease for my worry. Regardless, deep down inside, I knew that those were the only words they could say right then.

Still troubled, I tried to rest. More members of the family, and a few close friends began to show up. I welcomed the support, but was tormented by the repetition of the story. Sitting there as I listened to those words continually repeated to each new person was starting to take a toll on me. I had to get away, yet I still could not allow myself to go too far. After all, that's my big brother lying there across the hall.

Finally, run down and tired, I gave in and attempted to sleep. I made my way down the hall to a larger waiting room, found a couch, and collapsed.

Once again, I began to plead with the Lord. "Please save my brother! He has so much to live for, and so much more to do!" But mostly, my pleading with God was pure selfishness. I simply was not ready or willing to let him go. The only thought consuming me at that moment was of how much I needed him. He was my brother, my mentor, my hunting buddy, my inspiration, and one of my very few best friends. I needed him, and there was no way on earth I was remotely ready to let God take him from me! Completely exhausted, and mentally drained, I would spend the entire night pleading with God. Sleep would not come for me on August 25th.

3:00 am Thursday morning came much quicker than I expected after experiencing a restless night that seemed to never end. Groggy and sore, I left the small couch in the waiting room, and walked the long hallway to my brother's room. Quietly I brushed the door open and stepped in.

Lying before me was the man that just weeks before, was laughing and playing with my son back home at my parent's farm. To me, he hadn't changed. He still looked to be every bit of his strong and solid self. Every line on his beautiful face was exactly as I remembered it.

I stood at the foot of his bed for a minute and just stared at him. I watched him as a parent sometimes watches their newborn child sleep. It was almost surreal to watch. How could someone that had been through so much over the last few weeks be resting so peacefully, and be sleeping so soundly?

A wave of confidence rushed over me, and I knew right there he was going to be just fine. I walked to the head of his bed, and bent down beside him. I began to stoke his hair and whispered that I was there. His left eye opened and I again whispered to him. “Don’t try to talk.” I knew the blood clot on his lung made it difficult and painful to speak. The last thing I wanted was to cause him any more pain. I didn’t want him to try and answer any of my simple questions. I needed to keep it short and to the point.

Continuing to stroke his hair, I told him that I loved him, and that I have always known how much he loved me. I told him I knew he could beat this because I knew how strong he was. And with that, I leaned over and kissed his forehead. I told him again that I loved him, and that I needed to get going so I could try and make it to work on time.

I started to walk away, but for some reason turned back to get one more good look at him. As I did, I saw him slightly sit up in his bed. He coughed two times and raised his arm up to wave goodbye. I knew he was trying to say I love you, and it completely broke my heart. I waved back, told him I would see him later, and then quickly left his room. I wanted to stay so badly, but I couldn’t bear to have my big brother, see the great big tears that streamed down my face.

Psalm 119:50

Why?

Only by the grace of God was I able to make it to work on time August 26th. Despite my punctuality, I was of no value to my company for the majority of my morning there. Every minute that passed was nothing more than a foggy blur. Despite being completely exhausted and mentally drained I was there.

A number of hours passed, and my boss finally told me to go home and get some sleep. I remember getting back to my house around 11:00 am, and then stumbling my way up to my bedroom.

I awoke several hours later to see the clock reading 3:30 pm. Walking down stairs my wife greeted me. She told me that my Mother had given us a call while I was asleep. It seems that Clint had turned things around and was doing much better! He had gotten out of bed, he could talk, read from a book, and seemed to have all motor skills back. It was almost as if the stroke had never happened. It was a miracle!!!

I was completely relieved and feeling great! But little did I know, as the day would progress, things would begin to change for the worse. That Thursday night while I slept soundly in my bed, my big brother was in some of the worse pain of his entire life.

I woke Friday morning and began my normal routine. Shower, get dressed, quietly check on the kids, kiss my wife goodbye, and drive into work. But at 6:30 am as I sat at my desk doing paper work, my cell phone began to vibrate. My day was about to abruptly change.My heart sank, panic raced through my mind, and my stomach tied itself into an instant knot. I didn't want to answer since I knew there would only be bad news on the other end. No good news ever comes to my phone that early in the morning. Reluctantly, yet without hesitation, I answered. Jeff's wife Laurie is the voice that greets me on the other end. "Daniel... Clinton is not doing very well. They are taking him into surgery this morning so you may want to get here as soon as you can."

With out missing a beat, I flipped my phone closed and sprinted from my office. A hot cup of coffee sat abandoned on my desk, and my computer screen left glowing with budget information. In an instant, everything else became completely insignificant, and it seemed I could not leave that building fast enough.

I stopped off at my house for a quick change of clothing and to inform Sharon what was happening. I ran inside and was met by my wife and my son Reid at the door. Quietly I told Sharon what I was doing so I hopefully would not upset Reid with the bad news.

It's funny how observant a seven-year-old boy can be. Because right as I was ready to walk back out to my car, he walked up, quietly looked up at my face, and gave my waist a gigantic hug. He then looked back up at me, and with a voice of pure innocence said, "I really hope uncle Clint is going to be OK."

Wiping back my tears I did my best to comfort, and ease his mind. I told him that uncle Clint is a very strong person and is going to fight very hard for us. "However", I told him, "we still needed to pray very hard for him." Once again, I hugged them both and then left the house so I could start my long drive.

As I traveled down the road, panic raced through my mind. Never before had I been placed in a situation where I could possibly lose someone I loved so much. I began to pray and pray and pray... I really don't recall much else of that trip other than my constant prayers to please save my brother's life. I even found myself pleading with God, and begged him to have mercy on Clint's life.

Once again, I pull into the hospital that I had left not more than 30 hours before. Frantically I parked my car and raced to the waiting area across from Clint's room. I looked inside and asked if he was back from surgery yet. He wasn't. Actually, he never had gone in. Clint's health had rapidly turned and he became much to weak for the surgeons to operate. The doctors feared that if they took him in at this point, he would die on the operating table.

The following two hours were filled with questions, fears, and emotions I never dreamed I would have to experience. It was a continuous roller coaster ride. One minute the doctors had hope, the next they were preparing you for the worst. There was nothing I could do but wait and pray. I felt utterly helpless, and completely empty. It was one of the most horrific and wretched experiences I had ever faced.

Finally, after two hours of stomach churning turmoil, Caryn's two brothers convinced me to go eat lunch with them. At first I wanted to decline the offer. Eventually though, my voice of reason set in, and I knew I would need something more. After all, there still was a half finished cup of coffee sitting on my desk at work. Plus, there was a small piece of me hoping that maybe for a moment, it might take my mind off of things. I did go and eat, but try as I might, it seemed nothing could distract my thoughts.

We finished our lunch, and started our return to the waiting room. My dissatisfying lunch was not setting well with me as we made our way down the hallway, and back into the waiting room. Walking through the door we were met by the rest of my immediate and extended family. The door closed behind me, and I heard a strange voice ask if everyone is here now.

I turned, and sat on the corner of a couch, my eyes focused on a small statured man standing near the door. He looked at us all, and slowly began to speak. "Clint is not doing well... The blood clot in his aorta has stopped proper function of his kidneys, spleen, liver, and intestines." Then he paused for a second, and continued by saying: "I am just going to be very blunt with you. With all that has happened to Clint, there is no chance for survival left... The best thing you can do now is to go and be with him."

My heart sunk, and I instantly felt sick. My head was spinning, and I honestly had no idea what to do next. I was paralyzed as I sat there with an empty and stunned look on my face. I didn't want to listen anymore. Who was this man to give my brother a death sentence? He obviously did not know how strong Clint was! I would not accept that statement! And I was going to make certain Clint was not going to accept it either!

I rushed down the hallway to Clint's room as my family followed behind. Pushing through the door I focused on my big brother laying on his bed before me. He was sedated, and resting as if in an extremely peaceful sleep. He had no idea of the horrific and sickening words that had just been spoken. I moved to the side of his bed and began to stoke his hair. At first I had no idea what to say as I stood there with tears rushing down my cheeks. But then I knew. I had to help him fight. I needed him to prove those doctors wrong.

I bent down and kissed his forehead as I told him that I loved him. Behind me I could hear the rest of my family and two of our pastors begin to filter into the room. Slowly, one by one, people began to talk to Clint. They told him how much they loved him, and how they promised to help take care of his three beautiful children. But I was having none of that. I couldn't just give up like that! And I refused to let him give up either!

I moved to a chair in the corner of the room. Hanging my head and folding my hands I began to pray. "Lord Please... Save my brother... I need him!!!" I begged God to heal him, and to take away his pain and sickness. I remember pleading with God to help the doctor's figure something out. To simply find anything that may save his life. "Please Lord, grant me this one miracle!"

Looking back, I remember a point where I begged God to please use me. I would do what ever it took to help save my brother. I could give him my Kidney, or a bone marrow transplant. Pain and fear were of no consequence to me. I simply wanted my brother to be healed.

Slowly, the voices of those around me started to become clearer. My state of shock started to wear, and my feeling of sadness gave way to anger. How could everyone be giving up? I would not allow this! I stood up and walked back to my brother's bed. Leaning over him, I once again ran my finger through his short dark hair. I started to speak, but now my soft whispers had evolved into much more determined and urgent statements. "I know how strong you are. You cannot give up on me! I love you, and need you... COME ON BUDDY, YOU HAVE TO FIGHT HARD FOR ME!!!"

Fury began to run trough my veins. I wanted to turn and yell at everyone around me to just shut up! I want to scream at them! Stop telling him to let go! Stop telling him to run to Jesus, and to go with the angels! Don't they know how strong he is? Don't they know how much I need him? My head was spinning. I wanted to leave the room, but couldn't imagine leaving my brother's side.

Immensely distraught, I conceded to my need for a moment by myself. Rapidly I exited the room, and made my way down the hallway. Turning the corner, I found myself in the room where just two hours before, my heart had been ripped from my chest. There I stood, just staring through a window at the rooftop below me. I was angry, scared, exhausted, and alone.

Fumbling with my cell phone I decided to call my wife. I was torn. I wanted her with me, but also did not want to subject her to the pain engulfing me. Slowly, one by one, I pushed the numbers on the keypad and listened for the familiar voice.

It seemed as though she answered as soon as I pushed the last number. Her voice was trembling as she franticly told me how worried she had been. Her entire stress filled morning was spent wondering how things were going.

I told her things are not good, and that the doctors say he is not going to make it. Without missing a beat, I hear her say that she is coming. Her sister is going to drive her, and they are going to leave right now. I tell her I love her, and to please drive safely as I ended the call.

Once again I find myself torn with emotions. I long to feel the comfort of her loving arms holding me. Yet I want to protect her from witnessing the horrible reality of my brother slipping away.

My very next memory found me back in Clint's room. I don't recall walking there, in fact I don't recall walking throughout much of the afternoon that followed. I would find myself sitting on a chair in the corner of the room, my head bowed and hands folded as I prayed like never before. The very next minute I would find myself leaning onto Clint's bed as I held him in my arms.

I would repeat over and over that I knew how strong he was, and that he needed to fight for me! But never do I remember the process of moving from one spot to the other. I remember the countless family members and pastors as we huddled in that small room. I even remember hearing some of the words they spoke to Clint as he lay there before us. But for some strange reason, I never remember walking.

Looking at my watch I notice that it is now 4:00 pm, and I hear Clint's wife Caryn speak up. She asks the nurse if it would be OK to climb into bed beside Clint. As she lay beside him, I hear her broken voice as she address us all. "One of Clint's favorite songs was by Mark Schultz. In it there's a verse that talks about a husband who climbed into bed next to his dying wife so he could 'walk her home.' The song goes on to say how they were both happy since they knew it was not the end."

Hearing those words roll off of her lips made me proud, and yet in the same instant tore my heart into pieces. It was complete and utter torture for me. There was not one single thing I could do to stop any of this. Clint was slipping away, and all I could do was stand there and helplessly watch.

For the next hour, I leaned over his bed, and held him in my arms. Then at 5:00 pm on August 27th 2010, my big brother peacefully slipped away, and his beautiful spirit passed from this earth.

1Corinthians 15:54-57

Numb

Standing at the foot of Clint's bed, an inescapable fury raced through my body. Rage flowed through my veins, and I was smothered with a pain I had never before experienced. My head was spinning as anger, frustration, and confusion consumed me. How could this happen? Why did this happen? This cannot be a real experience I am living at this moment! The brother I loved so dearly just left me. And there I stood, feeling lost and alone.

Tears were streaming down my cheeks and shattering as they hit the hard tile floor. Then slowly, moment-by-moment, the storm inside me began to subside. My feelings of rage were starting to taper, and my chaotic fury gave way to an overwhelming despair as I stood paralyzed at the foot of his bed. At thirty-four years old, had I really reached the point where life stops giving and then begins to take away? I was numb and drowning in my sadness.

Somehow, I manage to break free from my paralysis, and move my stone-like legs. I made my way back up the side of Clint's bed, and once again leaned over to stoke his coarse dark hair. I whispered how much he meant to me, and again repeated my love for him. I told him that I promised to help take care of his three incredible children. I told him how proud of him I was, and how much I was going to miss him. But most importantly, I told him how I could never fully express the impact he had on my life. He was more than a brother, and much more than a friend.

Though I knew his spirit had left his body, I could not leave his side. I had to touch him. I had to stare at him. I wanted the image of his face burned into my memory. I was overcome with grief as I stood there beside him. Holding him, staring at him. I was not ready to let him go.

Moments later I was shaken from the haze engulfing me as Caryn once again addressed us all as she still lay in the bed beside Clint. Her words still echo in my mind and tug at my heart. Hearing her speak, I realized a pride for her that until then I had never known. She told us all that she would not allow there to be any separation of families in the following days. Her family and my family are not to go off and be by themselves. We were united through Clint, and we will stay that way regardless of whether he is here or not. Our families will be with each other, and stay with each other over these next difficult days, as well as all future days to come.

The room was slowly starting to clear. Family members were now starting to disperse so as to start the preparations for the next few days. Many decisions needed to be made. I however, could not be a part of helping to make them. I was in no mental place to even think about making them. All I could do was stand there and weep for my brother.

I'm not sure why, but something told me to look at my watch. I saw that it was 5:20 pm, and I realized my wife would be showing up soon. I told my parents I was going to find her, and that I would be back shortly. My father asked if on my way I would move his car, and Caryn's car from the parking garage. The Hospital was making repairs to that garage, and all cars needed to be moved by 6:00 pm or would be towed. I happily agreed to do so, and my parents pastor volunteered to help speed up the process.

We walked down the hall, rode the elevator, and made our way out to the front of the building. Neither one of us spoke a word. However, our silence had nothing to do with either of us not knowing what to say to each other. There are thousands of things we could have said. He could have tried to comfort me. I could have expressed my sadness. But looking back, I needed that silence, and I truly feel God allowed him to recognize that need.

We successfully move the cars across the street, and started our short walk back to the hospital. As we waited at the cross walk he finally broke the silence. His statement was short, simple and to the point. He did not try to comfort me, or give me words of wisdom. He simply looked at me and said:

"So it's been a pretty crappy week for you hasn't it." I responded with a "Yes, it most certainly has."

That was the end of our conversation, and quite frankly I'm glad it was. At that moment in time I did not need anything else. With those simple words he had acknowledge my pain. He was keeping things simple and speaking to me on my level. He could have quoted scripture, or tried to rationalize the situation with theology. But once again, I feel God spoke to him. I truly feel God allowed him to see me for who I was at that moment in time. Not the man I am today, but who I was then in that horribly painful moment.

The sentence that rolled off his tongue was an utterly simple statement, and honestly not one I had ever expected to hear from a pastor. Yet those brief and to the point words said it all. It had not only been a crappy day. It had been a crappy week. He recognized and acknowledged that for me. And quite honestly, sometimes it's just nice to know that people understand.

As we approached the front of the hospital, I saw the tall, slender figure of my wife as she walked through the front entrance with her sister. Not more than 30 yards behind her I began to pick up my pace, and quickly closed in on them. I finally caught up and called out to them as they were walking toward the elevator.

Hearing my voice, Sharon turned and walked back to me. Immediately she wrapped her arms around me and gave me the hug I had been longing for all day. As I was holding her tight, I heard the words: “I lost him” slip from my lips. Tears immediately began to stream down my cheek, and I buried my face into her soft blond hair. Standing in the middle of a crowded lobby I simply held my wife and cried.

We eventually made our way back up to Clint’s room so I could again be with my brother. It was quite wonderful to have her support while I was trying to deal with turmoil flowing through my mind. Finally, at 6:00 pm I came to the realization that I had to let him go. Completely exhausted, and an emotional wreck, I kissed his forehead and stoked his hair one last time. Then hand in hand, Sharon and I left his room.

Leaving the hospital, we ran into my oldest brother in the hallway. I told him I was exhausted and needed to go home. He hugged me and told me he loved me. He also told me how proud he was of me since he knew I was not a hospital kind of guy. He was right, as most of my hospital visits typically end with me passing out. Amazingly though, this time I somehow made it through.

As I turned to walk away, my second oldest brother Grant walked up. I told him that I was leaving, and then immediately gave him a hug. As I was hugging him, I whispered in his ear that I have always loved him just as much as I loved Clint. That was the first time that I can recall ever speaking those words to Grant. Not because I didn’t love him, or because there was tension between us. I was not lying when I said that statement to him. Grant and I have always gotten along. It’s just a simple fact that we are the two quiet ones in the family. We both have always known that we loved each other. I guess up until then, we both just figured that you don't need to say something when the other person already knows.

Sharon and I finally made it out to my car. She knew I was in no shape for driving, and asked me for the keys. Looking back, I can't begin to tell you how glad I am that she did. My mind was still racing, and the intensity of the day had left my body drained and exhausted. I was angry, heart broken, and smothered in confusion. I sat limp in my car as I gazed out the window and watched the yellow lines dash past me down the road. Slowly, mile-by-mile, I came to find myself in a very dark place.

2Corinthians 1:3-6

A Thick Fog

Saturday morning came, and Sharon, Reid, my daughter Kate, and I all got ready to make the trip home to my parent's farm. The ride was rather uneventful, and for the most part quiet. The kids were well behaved and Sharon allowed me to be alone with my thoughts. Surprisingly, it was quite a beautiful day for an August in Iowa. The sun was shining with few clouds, and the temperature was in the mid seventies with little to no humidity.

After reaching my parents house, we spent a little time gathering up various items and then drove over to Clint's house. The news of my brother's death had spread like wild fire, and already the tremendous outpouring of sympathy and support had started to show. Cars were parked all over the farmyard, and the house was filled with friends, family and neighbors. Some of which I hadn't seen in more than 20 years.

The farm that Clinton lived on was actually the farm that I had grown up on. (My parents did not move to their current farm until I was a Junior in High School.) I loved that old farm, and it meant the world to me that Clinton had moved back there. It was almost as if I was able to live vicariously through him. It was strange, but somehow by Clinton living there, I was allowed to enjoy that wonderful memory filled location for myself.

Spending the bulk of the next two days on that farm was actually somewhat bitter sweet for me. My brothers and I spent time walking around and reminiscing about all kinds of memories. The football games we played in the yard. Riding our motorcycles out in the tree filled grove. Various joys we had, and trouble we had gotten ourselves into. It was magical to be back there. But still we found a gaping hole inside each one of us. Most all of our memories had included Clint in one form or another, and it was a hard and simple fact that he simply was not there. He was missing out on our stroll down memory lane, and somehow that seemed to tarnish a piece of the joy from the moment.

Sunday afternoon came and I found myself sitting on the couch in Clint's living room. I was watching people scurry around as they tried to make last minute preparations for the funeral. The kids were outside playing with their cousins just as I had with my brothers and sister at that age. Occasionally I would catch a side conversation of a friend or family member. From time to time someone would sit down by me and ask how I was doing, but mainly I remember just sitting and thinking how none of this could be real. At some point Clint is going to walk through that door, and I will realize that it had all been some type of horribly twisted nightmare.

Suddenly a rather odd feeling flashed through my mind. There was an intense fire, and passion that rushed through my body. It was a feeling that I don't believe I have ever experienced before. I stood up from the couch, and walked over to a card table that had been set up in the middle of the room. Sitting down, I grabbed a piece of scratch paper and started writing. The words flowed effortlessly onto the paper as I sat there undistracted by everything around me. I was filled with an intense passion, and it seemed as if the words were almost breathed into me. The small scrap of paper quickly filled up, and I frantically scanned the room for something else to write on. I had so much to say and feared my thoughts might escape me.

Seeing a tablet on the desk across the room, I darted from my chair and scrambled over to grab it. I tore out a few pages and made my way back to sit at the small shaky table. My pen did not miss a beat as I wrote with ferocity and determination. The words still flowing through my fingers as they found their way down to the crinkled yellow paper. I had something important to say, I needed people to know my brother like I did. Who was he? What did he stand for? What was his legacy? Hopefully, I had answered some of those thoughts with the words I had just written. But even more importantly, I did not want those words to simply stay on those three crinkled sheets of paper. I wanted more people to experience them. I needed everyone else to know my brother as I did. In two short days I would have the chance to share those thoughts with a captive audience. It was those three word-filled sheets of paper that would eventually become the speech I gave at his funeral.

Monday morning came and our families gathered at the funeral home. This was a tough morning for me, as I am sure it was for everyone else. This is the day when reality sets in. You see the person you love so dearly as they peacefully lay in that silk lined coffin. Your mind is no longer allowed to play tricks on you. No longer are you able to try to tell yourself it's all a dream. This is reality, and it's lying right there before you.

In addition to the normal sadness of the situation, my morning would pose an additional mental challenge for me. My sister and I were asked to do Clint's hair for him. It's hard to describe my emotions that were attached to that task. On one hand it was a complete honor, yet still it was a completely agonizing experience. The process itself was easy, and to style it for him was very simple. Clint's coarse hair was awesome. It was an exquisite dark brown color that he always kept very short. In all actuality it styled itself, and there was very little I needed to do. To style it for him was simple; rub a dime sized glob of gel through your fingers, and then rake them forward a couple times through his scalp.

I touched his hair and immediately broke down. How could such a simple and honor filled task be so excruciatingly painful for someone to complete.

My sister looked at me and told me she could do it if I wanted her to. I shook my head no, and managed to spit out the words: "I can do this." With a few more strokes through his hair we were finished. I stood there for a few minutes and just stared at him. I reached down and touched his arm. Tears welling up in my eye, I was once again torn with emotion. I wanted to run away, but also couldn't leave his side. I wanted to speak to him, but didn't know what to say. Silently I stood there, simply touching his arm and gazing at his face.

Finally, I broke my silence with the only words it seemed my lips could form. Reaching over I placed my hand on his chest and whispered: "You have no idea how much I love you." With that I turned and left the room.

I made my way back out to the waiting area of the funeral home where the rest of the family was. There was only a few more that needed to arrive before we would all be ushered in and view Clint as a family. Waiting there, I again found myself filled with turmoil. This was not fair! We should not have to be here right now! I wanted to be angry with someone, but who was I to blame? Who are we to question God's plan for us? All I could do was stand beside my wife and hold her as I tried to find some comfort in her touch.

Caryn and the three kids entered the room first and were allowed some time by themselves. A short while went by, and the rest of us were allowed to filter into the room. Even though I had seen his body less than 20 minutes before, it still was hard for me to walk back up to that coffin and look down on him.

There I was. Looking down on my brother as tears filled up my eyes. My two other brothers made their way over and the three of us silently stood before the man we loved so much. The four brothers were back together again, but it wasn't as it should be. Even though only one of us had fallen, three of us had been hurt, and this time there was no band-aid or ice pack that could fix our pain. We each had come to discover that there was now a gaping hole in us that would never be filled. There we stood. We were silent, and we cried.

Psalm 5:1-3

Not Completely Blind

Toward the end of our time at the funeral home, my father stepped up beside me as I stood looking down on Clint. He put his arm around me and began to once again bestow his wisdom on me. He knew how much I loved him, and could see how much I hurt. His words were simple and to the point. He acknowledged my pain, and did his best to comfort me. But the most wonderful thing he did for me that day was to help me start opening my eyes.

I'm sure he did not even realize the impact he was having. Here a loving father was simply trying to comfort his hurting son. But in the midst of his love, he was also teaching. He was not allowing me to dwell on my pain, or wallow in my anger. Here was a man that had been dealt the same unfair hand. Yet he was overlooking the pain and focusing on the purpose. While feeling a pain that matched my own, he was taking my hand and attempting to guide me.

The words he spoke were simple, yet elegantly placed. They didn't form a drawn out speech, or some type of in-depth rationalization. They were simply the words I needed to hear, but more importantly they were spoken with the love I needed to feel. I am grateful for every word my father spoke to me that day, but it was the words he quoted from James 4:14 that would help start my journey.

For those of you not familiar with this Bible verse it reads: "Yet, you do not even know what tomorrow will bring. What is your life? For you are a mist that appears for a little while and then vanishes."

Far be it from me to interpret the word of God, but that doesn't mean I wont try. For me, this verse is teaching us that this life is not ours. It's not in our hands, and it's not up to us as to how long or short it will be. Ultimately, God's plan for our lives lies completely in his hands. It is his will, not ours. The life we know here on earth is but a breath of air when compared to our eternal life in heaven. Only God can decide how long or short that breath will be.

Even with those awesome words of incredible wisdom, I still found it hard to function that day. It would be numerous days before that insight would resonate, and finally make sense. The pain and anger I was feeling was fogging my mind, and was not allowing me to see the beauty of my brother experiencing the joys of heaven. I was slowly sinking in a sea of selfishness, and was consumed with self-pity. I no longer had the brother I loved so dearly, and it seemed there was no consoling me.

That evening the visitation for Clint was held in the high school gymnasium as they expected a very high turnout. I began the night reluctant and reserved. I didn't want to be there. I didn't want to be in the midst of thousands of people, some of which I had never met before in my life. I didn't want to look at the distress and pain on the faces of everyone in my family. And for some reason I didn't want to have complete strangers telling me how sorry they were for me. I was sorry enough for myself, and didn't need the constant reminder of what I had lost. I was a wreck, and at that moment in time I didn't want to be surrounded by hundreds of faces I didn't know. Was the sorrow they expressed sincere? Would the river of tears ever stop flowing from my eyes? I could feel my anger and selfishness begin to rear its' ugly head, and once again I had come to find myself in a very dark place.

The remainder of the night was a roller coaster of emotions for me. I can't count the number of times I had to retell the story of the previous week for people that questioned how all of this happened. Every word I spoke forced me to relive those horrible days, and each one that rolled off my tongue would become more painful than the last. I knew everyone's intentions were innocent. They simply wanted to understand. They needed some form of closure regardless of how small it may be. So, reluctantly I would retell the story time and time again. It was agonizing and stressful, but still there was a small piece of me that hoped after telling it enough times, it would eventually get easier. Nonetheless, what I found was that it only made me hurt that much more.

The night wore on as I slowly found myself becoming increasingly numb to the situation. Hour after hour time slipped away, and I felt myself deteriorating. Numerous people told me how they came to support me, but found themselves being the one receiving the support. They were in awe of my family's strength through the situation, and were shocked by the role reversal, as we were now the ones comforting them.

For some reason though, that thought did not sit well with me. What those people saw in me was not real. I wasn't strong. I was a complete mess. Every negative adjective in the dictionary couldn't begin to describe the utter despair I was experiencing. When people looked at me, they were not actually seeing resilience. What they were witnessing was a guise, a mere ploy, a simple act of smoke and mirrors. The fact that I had stopped crying was simply due to being dehydrated. I had no tears left to cry even though I desperately wanted to. My stoic demeanor was nothing more than me mentally checking out from the situation. The people around me were not witnessing strength. They were witnessing a lie.

Psalm 116:1-8

What Now?

Tuesday was the day of my brothers funeral, and it came much too quickly for me. That morning I awoke to the sound of a steady and somewhat heavy rainfall. There was no thunder, no lightning, and no strong winds. It was nothing more than a simple and steady rain. Oddly enough, it was actually quite beautiful. To me, it almost seemed as if God was crying the tears I was unable to produce the night before. I loved it! It seemed as though he was speaking to me. He was using the rain as a metaphor if you will. With every drop that ran down the pane of glass on the window, God was washing away my hurt and my sorrow. He was cleansing me from my anger and despair.

It was quite magical, but yet it would become even more profound in the following moments. Because the minute my wife and I stepped out the door and lifted our umbrella, the rain instantly stopped. Had I not seen it with my own eyes, I would have never believed it. It was a very small act that could have been easily overlooked or dismissed. But to me, it was amazing! God was making his presence known. He was grabbing me by the shoulders and shouting at the top of his lungs: "Look who's in control... It's not you!"

Sharon and I finished our walk down the driveway to our car with out one drop of rain ever touching our heads. It was quite a surreal experience to have witnessed, despite how small it may seem. It was absolutely awesome, and much bigger than a coincidence.

We arrived back at the school, and made our way inside to find the rest of our family. The funeral director had a few questions for us, and then informed us of the process and schedule for the funeral itself. He then informed us that everyone else would be arriving shortly, and that now would be our chance to spend a few last private moments with Clint.

I quickly left the room, as I needed to see him one more time. I needed one more brief moment with his body. I wanted to touch him and stare at his face. How are you supposed to say goodbye to someone you have loved and looked up to your entire life? How do you accept the fact that someone who shouldn't be leaving is now gone?

I was struggling with those thoughts, and had absolutely no idea what the answer should be. But as I stood there looking down on the brother who meant the world to me, I prayed to God. I asked him to please somehow help me find some clarity in it all. Help me to understand and to give me the strength I needed to move forward.

With the end of my prayer and tears streaming from my eyes, I bent down and kissed my brothers forehead. I then stood back up and touched his arm as I told him how deeply I loved him. I told him how blessed I was to have been his brother, and how lucky I was to have experienced him in my life. With tears still flowing, I reached up and touched his dark hair one last time. And with that, I turned and walked away.

Upon arriving back in the room I sat down next to my wife and began to edit the speech I had planned to give. Again I had a fire inside me. In fifteen short minutes I rewrote all three of the pages that I had penned just two days before. It needed to be right. I had to make sure everyone knew who he was. I wanted them to know him like I did.

The time had finally come, and they escorted us to our seats. Walking to my chair, I was taken aback and completely awe struck as I passed row upon row of a sea of faces. It was inspiring and uplifting to see the mass of people that had come to pay honor and respect to Clint. But even more amazing, was the fact of knowing that he had somehow personally touched each one of those individuals' lives. It was an awesome and dumbfounding sight to have witnessed.

The funeral began and I found a rather unusual calmness washing over me. I was still consumed by an overwhelming sadness, and chaotic hurt deep in my soul. Both of which were easily explained by an unshakeable selfishness of not wanting to be without my brother, but the calmness was a strikingly unexpected gift from God.

Both Pastors that day shared truly beautiful addresses. Both were inspiring, heartwarming, and an incredible tribute to my brother. My sister and oldest brother also shared uplifting and amazing words to honor Clint's life and memory. It goes without saying that I was proud of every word spoken that day. More importantly, I was elated with the thought that so many individuals had the opportunity to witness those words describing the beautiful life and man who was my brother.

If I may however, I would like to share with you the words that I spoke to the crowd that day. Not because I feel my speech was more profound or enlightened than any one else's, or because I am overly proud of it. Simply put, the words I wrote struck a cord in my own heart. I feel they are a simple perspective of who my brother was, and what he meant to me. More so, I feel they are a striking example of how we should strive to be the type of person, friend, brother, and son that he was.

Bear with me as you read the following speech. It's a quick read, and far from upper brow. Regardless, I hope you find it to be more than a string of heartwarming words. I hope that you can open your heart and mind, and are able to read between the lines. Most of all I pray that you are able to use it as an eye opening push toward trying to be the same individual that he was.

"Clinton"

In the midst of everything that took place over the last number of days, I started to look back and find all those special things that helped make Clinton who he was. While I reflected on them all, there was one thing that really stood out to me. Whether you knew it or not, Clint was a teacher long before he had that little slip of paper that said he could do it for a profession. Being lucky enough to have spent 34 years with him, I could stand here for hours upon end and tell you stories, share memories, and cite lessons learned. But for the sake of you all, I'll pick out a few special ways he was a teacher to me that will always resonate in my mind.

I still remember the countless times we would drive into town, and make our way down to one of the dime stores on Main Street. Inevitably the two of us would end up in the candy aisle, and before I knew it, Clint was handing me 10 cents and a green Jolly Rancher stick as he pushed me toward the counter so I could pay for him. To many siblings this would be a rather annoying thing, but to me he was teaching. He was teaching this shy little boy to have confidence and courage. But most importantly he was teaching me to be a selfless servant.

The other thing that stands out is how well he knew me. Even at a young age he knew that by telling me I couldn't do something, would make me mad enough that I would only want to do it even more! He knew that I would try even harder simply to prove him wrong. The amazing thing about that was he always knew exactly when to play that card. I know that because I can't even begin to count the number of times that he was the first one in line telling me that I could do something, and that he wasn't going to let me quit. What was my lesson learned? Get to know the people in your life well enough so that you know the best way to motivate and support them.

Like I said, I could go on and on for hours. But to spare you all from my incoherent rambling, I'll end with these two thoughts.

One of the wisest men I know once told us boys to never miss an opportunity to tell someone you love them. And praise the Lord I was lucky enough to do just that with Clinton. Life is short and precious. You can't go through it with the impression that the people around you know exactly how you feel about them. Make sure you always speak the words! Because you never know when your opportunity to do so will be gone.

> *Last thing... If you forget everything else I say today, I want you to remember this one thing about Clint. The brother he was, helped make me the man I am. Even though most of you weren't lucky enough to call him a brother, you can still think about him and realize this: the man he was, helped make the person you are. My hope is that you can take the gift he gave you, and pass it on to someone who wasn't lucky enough to know him.*
>
> *I love you Clint, and I will never forgot what you've done for my life.*

As the funeral service was ending, and my family was ushered from the auditorium. The song "This Life" by MercyMe began to play over the speaker system. If you ever get the chance, I highly recommend taking the time to listening to it. Not only do I feel it is a completely triumphant and uplifting song, but the words are completely fitting with what our attitudes toward this earthly life should be. In my mind it was the perfect ending to Clint's funeral. That incredible song not only shows us who we should be, but also summarizes who Clint was, and what he was all about.

My next solid memory of that day found me standing in the cemetery. The door to the hearse opened, and the six of us boys stepped up to move Clint's casket. Jeff, Grant, and myself stood on one side, and Clint's three brother-in-laws on the other. What an honor to be given! But yet what a whirlwind of emotions associated with such a task. It's hard to put words on the feelings one experiences when you are carrying your brother to his final resting place. On one hand there is an overwhelming sense of pride, but on the other hand you are overrun with sadness and grief. It was one of the hardest things I've ever had to do, and yet would do it again in a heartbeat if asked.

The six of us boys fulfilled our task, and the pastor once again spoke with wisdom and beauty. But the most heart warming and honor filled instant of that entire moment in time was witnessing one of my brothers wishes come true. Clint had always said that at his funeral he wanted the song "Amazing Graze" to be played by bagpipes. Think what you will about the sound that emanates from that distinctive Scottish instrument. But let me tell you first hand, I have yet to hear a more beautiful sound than the one that day in the cemetery.

The end of the funeral marked a pinnacle of confusion for me. Family and friends lingered for a while. Numerous hugs and tears were shared, and countless kind words were spoken. But something just wasn't right with me. I took a moment and slipped over to Clint's coffin. Standing there I placed my hands on top of it and began to speak to him. My words and the promises I made are private, but I did express the overwhelming love, respect, and pride I had for him. However, it wasn't until I began to see everyone leaving that my confusion set in.

As I stood there with tears rolling down my cheeks a strange thought came over me. "What now? Is this all there is? We live our life, we die, and then some people show up to our funeral. Then what? Does everyone just leave and go on with their normal life as if nothing ever happened?" My thoughts were not based on if there is a heaven or hell, my thought was strictly based on the individuals who come to show their support. Did they take anything away from this experience? Had they learned anything from witnessing the life my brother lived? Will knowing Clint change them the same way it has changed me?

The confusion that raced through my mind only compounded the complete sadness I was living at that moment. I was wallowing in self-pity, and blinded by my tortured heart. I thought I needed to be comforted, and I thought I needed to get past my pain and my grief. But what I truly needed was for God to open my eyes, and grant me the wisdom to find the answers that were eluding me.

Proverbs 16:1-9

Starting To See

The Saturday following Clint's funeral found me sitting in the bleachers at the Central College football game. Jeff is the head coach of the team, and I went to show my support for him on his opening game of the season. It was a gorgeous day and absolutely perfect weather for a football game. I stood there in a sea of people trying my best to focus on the game, but try as I might; I still was not able to pull my mind away from Clint.

Partway though the first quarter, my mom and dad had finally made it to the stadium, and I saw them making their way through the bleachers to the seats next to mine. My dad took the seat immediately to my left, and my mom sat next to some friends a few seats to my right. We watched for a while, and eventually my dad leaned over and asked if I was handling everything ok. I meekly responded with a yes, and nodded my head in agreement. The truth however, was that I hadn't been handling everything very well. I didn't feel fine, and I didn't think that everything was going to be ok.

I knew I shouldn't lie about something like that. Especially not to my father, but somehow in my mind I was attempting to spare everyone else from any added stress in their lives. Everyone around me had enough grief and worries of their own. The last thing anyone needed was to have the burden of worrying about my mental state added to their already overflowing concerns. Besides, I could handle any depression and sadness on my own; right?

I am guessing that my dad read into my response, and assumed that I truly wasn't doing fine. Just like any good parent can tell when their child is lying to them, I'm sure my father could see right through mine. Despite his own hurting and grief, he took the time to reach out and yet again offer some enlightenment and wisdom on the subject.

Sitting there as the second quarter of the game played out, he shared with me the devotion he had read that morning. He told me how it was quite amazing how God had placed the devotional before him, and had then allowed him to see the meaning behind it. As I sat there and listened to him, I too understood the amazing work of God's hand as well.

The basis of the devotion was about members of the military, or warriors if you will. Through it the author explains how sometimes these warriors will die in sacrifice to uphold what it is they are fighting for. Just like members of the military, there are also warriors for Christ who will pay the ultimate sacrifice as well. The difference between these two is that while the military is fighting a foreign adversary who wants to destroy their country, warriors for Christ are fighting Satan who wants to destroy the souls of everyone on earth.

To additionally juxtapose these two; we need to look no further than the topic of casualties. Just like a casualty on the battlefield, sometimes there are casualties in spiritual battles as well. One life may have been lost when a member of the military was killed on the battlefield, but look at how many lives were saved back home through the death of that individual fighting for their freedom. Equally the same, warriors in Christ may loose their earthly lives, but have still made an impact on countless other people by shining the light of God while they were still among us.

In battle when a soldier is killed, those around that individual are filled with emotion. Some are sad, some are angry. But despite how those closest to him feel, the sacrifice that person made will make a difference in the lives of everyone else. Whether you are consciously aware of it or not, every member of the military is fighting for you and me on a daily basis. Warriors for Christ are no different.

Everyday that passes, warriors for Christ are fighting for all of us, but instead of fighting for the freedoms we have in this country; warriors in Christ are fighting for our spiritual freedom. Clint was no stranger to that daily fight. Just look at the number of lives he was able to touch every single day. The children in his classroom, the boys on his track team, and the family members around him; he was fighting for us all. Looking at the death of my brother through this context makes it easy to see that Clint was most definitely one of those warriors!

I left the game that day feeling a little better, but even still, everything that God was trying to reveal to me had not fully sunk in. I was still hurting, and still slightly depressed. For some reason despite the help of my family and friends, I just could not shake that stabbing pain of sadness that engulfed me.

The next week passed, and I simply could not shake my intense feelings of sorrow. I tried to dive into my work thinking that keeping busy may take my mind away from my sadness. I tried to talk with my friends and family and express the anger that was welling up inside me. But try as I might, nothing seemed to work.

I felt alone and scared as I watched the dark fog once again approaching my life. I needed to overcome my anger and depression. I needed to understand the meaning behind all of this. I needed God to open my eyes and grant me the wisdom to see the purpose in my pain. I desperately needed a revelation!

I was frantic, and feared I may never find comfort for my crippling pain. Somehow though, deep down in my soul, I knew that the only true answers I would find would have to come from God.

That weekend I took some time for myself and drove around town while I ran some errands. While driving from destination to destination, my male instincts kicked in and I began the typical channel surfing on my car's radio.

As I flipped through the various channels I landed on 107.1, which is the local Christian radio station. I had listened to that station before, but that morning as I hit those call numbers, I was stopped dead in my tracks. The song that drifted across my car's speakers was a song by the group MercyMe.

This was not just any old song; this was one of the main songs sung at Clint's funeral. MercyMe was one of Clint's favorite groups, and the song "I Can Only Imagine" was one of his favorite songs. Hearing the words to that song resonate through my car caused me to completely break down. Tears were overrunning my eyes and streaming down my cheeks. Eventually I had to pull into a nearby parking lot as the tears that were drowning my eyes, had begun to inhibit my driving ability.

Sitting there with tears streaming down my face, something clicked in me. It was as if there was a little voice in my head prompting me with questions. I began to wonder what exactly was causing me this type of reaction? Is it simply the connection I have between this song and Clint's funeral? Or was it deeper than that? Are the words and the meaning of this song pulling at my heart and opening my mind?

There had to be more to all of this, and it was imperative that I find out. There was a reason Clint loved all of the musical groups he did, and it was much bigger than a band that could offer a catchy tune or toe-tapping beat. The groups he loved offered meaning and insight through their songs, and I needed to discover that for myself as well.

Wiping back my remaining tears and regaining my composure, I drove directly to the Christian bookstore in town. I quickly entered in and began to browse through the vast selection of CDs available. As my eyes scanned the racks, I searched my mind for the artists I knew Clint enjoyed. Slowly one by one the names came back to me: Mark Schultz, Casting Crowns, Third Day, MercyMe, News Boys, and countless others. I quickly made my selection of three different discs and made my way up front to pay. An air of excitement washed over me, and I was extremely eager to listen to every song that awaited my ears.

Racing out to my car, it seemed as though I couldn't unwrap the packaging fast enough. I was a child on Christmas morning, and the remnants of the plastic wrappers began to fall scattered at my feet. I placed the first disc in and hit play as I began to drive back home, but before the first song from the Casting Crowns' CD could finish, my cell phone rang, and I was forced to turn down the volume.

I finished the call as I pulled into the driveway of my home having missed hearing the majority of the CD I just purchased. Knowing that I had work in the house to complete that day, and a couple small children who were eager to play with their daddy,

I turned off the car and decided that the CD could wait for my trip back to work Monday morning.

The remainder of the weekend flew by, and before I realized what was happening, I found myself awakened to the sound of my alarm clock screaming at me to get out of bed. Like every Monday morning, 4:30 came much too early. I forced myself from the warm pile of covers that I had burrowed into, and quickly danced across the cold floor of my bathroom to turn on the shower. Still groggy and needing to stretch my sore muscles, I hopped in the shower and unknowingly began a day I will never forget.

I finished up my normal routine and made my way down to the garage where I was reminded of the new CD's that were waiting for me in the car. I hopped in and started down the street as I restarted the Casting Crowns disc I had been unable to finish two days earlier. The words and melody were wonderfully addicting and I found myself listening more intently than I have ever listened to a CD before. It was completely invigorating, and honestly one of the best starts to a workweek I had ever experienced.

Then something amazing happened as I neared my office. Exiting the interstate and turning to the East, I could just make out the beginnings of the sun breaking the horizon. The beams of light were just beginning to dance across the crest of the earth, as track number six began to play. It was a beautiful moment granted by the hand of God, but it was made even more beautiful by what God was about to reveal to me.

Track number six on the Casting Crowns CD "The Alter and the Door" is their title track. As I drove down that road, and heard the words to that song, a switch was flipped in my soul. Something clicked, and it all began to make sense. God spoke to me that morning at 5:30 as I drove down that dark and winding road. And it was utterly amazing!

God was not simply taking his hand and touching my heart. He was grabbing me by the shoulders and shaking me from my sleep! It was as if God was shouting at me: "Listen up dummy! It's not about you... It's about Me!!!"

I am forever grateful to Casting Crowns for the words to that beautiful song. More so, I am eternally grateful that God placed that song in my life at just the right time. Had I heard it a year before, it may have just been another catchy tune, and all meaning would have been lost.But in that one brief moment God opened my eyes. He granted me the wisdom to bring things into perspective. He had a completely captive audience with me as I drove down the road, and he used that moment to his advantage.Just as God had a captive audience with me, so do I have one with you as you read this book. With that said, I would like to share the first verse from that Casting Crowns song that impacted me so deeply.

"The Alter and the Door"

Careless, I am reckless
I'm a wrong-way-traveling' slowly-unraveling shell of a man
Burnt out, I'm so numb now
That the fire's just an ember way down in the corner of my cold, cold heart
Lord, this time I'll make it right, here at the alter I lay my life
Your kingdom come but my will was done, my heart is broken as I...
Cry, like so many times before
But my eyes are dry before I leave the floor,
Oh Lord I try
(I'll try)
But this time, Jesus, how can I be sure I will not lose my follow through
Between the alter and the door

Maybe as you read through those lines, you found that the words Mark Hall wrote were just as profound for you as they had been for me. You too may feel that you're a numb and burnt out shell of a man. Or possibly your cold and broken heart has caused you to travel in the wrong direction. Yet despite your constant promises to make things right with the Lord, your follow through of those promises never seem to follow you out the doors of the church.

If you found yourself relating to any of those thoughts or feeling, then listen to these next words.

It doesn't have to be that way! Stop living the lie, and start living for God! God has an extremely important message for us all. He is always there to offer his love and support for us even in our most trying of times! God is the one that can pick us up and dust us off whenever we fall, regardless of how many times it may happen. He is the one who can forward us the strength we need to make good on our follow through. For it's only though him that we will truly be able to open our eyes.

Trust me when I say that it is a strikingly incredible thing to have your eyes opened by God. The perspective you realize and knowledge that flows forth is quite honestly hard to explain. So many different things were revealed to me that beautiful September morning. In that one pivotal moment of time, answers were revealed to me that I feared I never would find. I wrestled with thoughts and cried for days following my brother's death. The struggles and questions that passed though my mind only added to the turmoil I felt in my soul. However, in one short instant, and with one beautiful song, God had spoken to me. He opened my eyes, and granted me the answers that had been eluding me. Clint was the warrior my father had spoken of a little over a week before. He was my warrior... My brother had died in order to save *my* life!

Psalm 43:2-5

Eyes Wide Open

Please don't misunderstand my words. By no means am I comparing my brother to Jesus. No, Clint did not die to save me from my sins. But God did use Clint's death to solidify my eternal place in heaven. When God opened my eyes, I was able to see things so much more clearly. I was able to look back at my life and realize things that I had overlooked as simple moments in time. Except now I could actually put real meaning behind them.

A perfect example of this was a memory I shared with Caryn while the two of us were at the funeral home standing by Clint's coffin. As the two of us stood there and cried looking down on my brother, a thought popped into my head that I felt the need to share with her.

The summer months of growing up on an Iowa farm would always find numerous opportunities of work that needed to be done in the field. One such task was to walk through the soybean fields and cut out any weeds that may be growing between the rows. Since it will take quite a few days to walk 300 acres of bean, you can only imagine the amount of stories, jokes, and questions that would drift about the beans.

It just so happened that one of those hot summer days; Clint and I were walking one of the south 80-acre fields with Bret Engelkes, who was a friend of ours from high school. All of the normal teenage boy conversations and jokes had been taking place when of course the obvious talk about girls came up. I vividly remember Bret asking Clint which of the girls from our school he liked. Without missing a beat Clinton looked back at Bret and told him he was planning on asking out that Caryn Rose girl.

I never understood why I always remembered that moment in time until my eyes were opened and everything came into view for me. I hadn't just witnessed my brother begin his journey of falling in love with his future wife. I had witnessed the beginning of my brother's life coming full circle. You see it was *walking* through a bean field in the middle of Iowa that I watched my brother decide to fall in Love with Caryn. And it was standing in an overcrowded hospital room that I witnessed my sister-in-law *walk* my brother home. God can reveal some pretty cool things when you allow him to open your eyes.

However, I must offer a word of warning to anyone who shares my prayer of opening your eyes. Because when God does grant you that beautiful gift, you may just find there are things you don't like to see. I should know because just such a subject was revealed to me that morning in

September when God used that incredible song to open my eyes, and speak to my heart.

It was a wake up call that I never would have expected at 5:30 in the morning, but you never really know when God will work in your life. Hearing those words in that song made me realize that I was the man Mark Hall was singing about. How many times had I found myself burnt out, numb, and traveling the wrong way? How many days had I ended up in church with tears in my eyes, and no fire in my heart? How many instances was it my will, not the Lord's that was done? More importantly, how many times had I promised that this time I would make it right, only to lose my follow through between the altar and the door?

It can be quite the punch in the stomach when God reveals to you how wrong you've been. God definitely knows how to take the wind out of your sails when you're lost at sea and heading the wrong direction. But the incredible thing is that by stopping the wind, he's not delivering a punishment; he's actually offering his help. You just need to open your eyes and recognize the help he's offering.

Yes my friend, he may have stopped the wind from blowing, but that was simply to make you look down and realize your compass is broken. You were adrift in the wrong direction, and he needed to put you back on course. God will always offer the opportunity; but it's up to you and me to offer the follow through.

My compass was broken, but I wasn't paying attention. The waves of the ocean had tossed me in the wrong direction, and I never even realized it. Had Clint not died, I firmly believe that I would have continued my life lost at sea. That's not to say I was a bad person, or that I wasn't a Christian. I simply had become too comfortable, and my Christian life was suffering. The best way I can explain this is through one of my favorite speeches I often give to help motivate and encourage my employees at work. The following words are from that very speech.

"Complacency"

I know that many of you out here are very much into sports. I also know many of you understand the ins and outs of the different honors someone can receive when they participate in college athletics. Because of that you know one of the highest honors a college athlete can gain is the rank of "All American." However, what you may not know is that back in the day when I was running college track, I actually had the opportunity to gain that title for myself. Not only did I have that opportunity, it was easily within my reach. You see, I was the lead leg of a 4X400 team that was ranked 8th in the nation.

Going into the National Track and Field meet it seemed as though the four of us boys just needed to show up and do what we had been doing all year long. We had already proven time and time again that we were capable, so what was going to stop us this time? It sounded rather simple, show up at the

University of Nebraska, run a 48 second split, and go home with the title of All American.

But we over looked one big problem. That problem was a horrible little word called complacency. We showed up at the University of Nebraska, but we showed up with the wrong attitude. We walked through those doors with the wrong mindset. And instead of going home with the great honor of All American, we simply went home with a great big broken heart. It was nothing more than two hundredths of a second that crushed our dream, and there wasn't anything we could do but walk off the track and watch our goal slip through our fingers. We had no one to blame but ourselves. We had become complacent, and failed miserably because of it.

My point here is not to try and have you compare your job to becoming an All American. What I am asking though, is that you challenge yourself to not allow that same horrible word creep into your life. You cannot allow yourself to become complacent in your job. It's imperative that you start each and every day striving to make this one better than the last. Look to this day and use my failure as a warning for what may be waiting for you today. Recognize it, overcome it, and then help others to defeat it as well.

I have always been proud of that speech, and have used it time and time again with countless different employees. However, what I failed to realize was that I had once again become the epitome of what I warned so many others to avoid. I had reverted back to defining the word that I had told so many others to despise. The difference this time was that I had not become complacent about my ability to run fast. I had become complacent in my Christian life. I was simply going through the motions and my eternal salvation was in jeopardy.

You may not like what you see when God opens your eyes, but it's no different than looking in a mirror. If you don't think the outfit you're wearing flatters you, go change! God opened my eyes and allowed me to look in his mirror. He used Clint's death to save my life. Not my earthly life, but my eternal life. My prayer for you is that God forwards you the same opportunity to look in his mirror. You'll want to look closely though, because you may just find that my brother Clint died for you too.

Luke 22:31-32

20/20 Vision

My brother was awesome! You couldn't ask for a better brother, father, husband, friend, teacher, coach or Christian. So why was it that God took him away from us? Isaiah 57:1-2 states that: "The righteous shall perish, and no one takes it to heart; the devout are taken away, and no one understands that the righteous are taken away to be spared from evil. Those who walk uprightly enter into peace; they find rest as they lie in death."

Was my brother being spared from the evils of this world? Possibly, but I'm not sure that's 100% of the reason. Just as I am not sure that his death was solely used to serve in opening *only my eyes*. Honestly, none of us will ever be 100% sure until we ourselves are called to heaven. With that said though, I still firmly believe that God uses pain and turmoil in our lives for good purposes.

In the days following my brother's death, I had countless people tell me that even though it makes no sense as to why someone so young and vibrant had to die, we still can not question God's plan. I disagree with that statement. I actually think it is quite the opposite. I think God wants us to question him. You just need to make sure you're questioning him for the right reason. In other words, what's your motivation for doing so?

Are you questioning his omniscience by trying to tell him that you know better? If that's your motivation, then you are completely wrong! However, if your questions are ones of searching for enlightenment, then you are on the right track. I truly believe that God wants us to question him. He just wants us to ask the right questions.

Think back to when you were in grade school. Did you not have to ask the teacher questions in order to find out the answers? How about the small child that runs to their parent and asks how something works, or where something comes from? Does the loving parent deny them a response? Absolutely not, and God is no different! His response may not be immediate, and there is no guarantee we will like the response that is given. But make no mistake; he will eventually answer us. For it is through his answers that we become stronger Christians, and that ultimately leads us closer to his loving arms.

God's answers are also not simply limited to our questions. Whenever we look at God providing us answers, we must also look at our requests of him. Whether we're asking a question or requesting his help, we are ultimately still looking for an answer from him. Both instances we are simply asking him for something, and then waiting for an answer. Regardless of our approach, his response to us will always follow the same guidelines. It may not be immediate, we may not like what we hear, and we may not understand why he told us what he did. He will however, always answer.

A perfect example of this is the day my brother passed away. I sat in that hospital and I prayed and pleaded with God to heal my brother. I begged him to take away his pain and cure him from his sickness. He answered my prayer that day, it just wasn't answered the way *I thought* it should have been. You see I wanted to be in control. I thought that I knew better than God, and that he needed to answer my prayer by curing my brother of his Leukemia. But God knew better.

He most certainly answered my prayers, and he fulfilled all my requests. He simply did it on his terms, not mine. Yes, God healed my brother, and he removed his pain better than any doctor ever could have. You see, God welcomed my brother home to heaven where there is no pain, no tears, or sickness. God answered my prayers, and he most certainly healed my brother. I was just too blind to see it at the time.

When we are faced with troubling or trying times in our lives, it is imperative we realize that there are always two main choices we have to decide between. We can become bitter, reclusive, and angry with God, or we can call on him to help us find the answers of how to utilize the obstacles in our life. You must pay close attention however as Satan will also be waiting for you there. You must remember the Devil loves nothing more than to plant doubt and anger in your heart.

Satan's number one goal in our lives is to drive an irremovable wedge between God and us. He finds complete joy in leading us as far away from God as he can.

One such way he succeeds at separating us from God is by misleading us to believe that the prayer we just poured our heart into has fallen on deaf ears. He did just such a thing with me as I prayed for God to please cure my brother. He was able to creep into that hospital room and plant a seed of doubt in my mind. If God was omnipotent, why did he not save my brothers life? Take a look at Mark 9:24. Jesus himself stated: "All things can be done for the one who believes." What about Matthew 26:53 where we again find Jesus making the bold statement: "Do you think that I cannot appeal to my father, and he will at once send me more than twelve legions of angles?"

Where were God's answers to my prayers? Where were my legions of angles when I needed them? I had poured my heart and soul out to God and it seemed as though he had turned his back on me. Or at least that is what Satan wanted me to believe. Where we fail as humans is thinking that we see an unanswered prayer, or the absence of God. When what we should actually see is the plan of God.

You need to look no further than the remainder of Matthew 26 to realize this for yourself. My problem was that Satan had me stop reading at verse 53 when I should have continued through verse 54. Had I not stopped at verse 53, I would have heard

Jesus finish his statement by saying: "But how then would the scriptures be fulfilled which say it must happen this way?"

Jesus got it! He was able to see and understand God's plan regardless of the horrific turmoil that awaited him. In that moment, it could have been strikingly easy for Jesus to see the absence of his father, but he didn't. His eyes were wide open and he saw the plan that God had in place for him.

We must approach our own trying times in the exact same fashion. We must trust that God has a purpose for our pain. We cannot allow Satan to mislead us, and then trick us into stopping short at verse 53. It is utterly crucial that we maintain 20/20 vision and read all the way through verse 54.

Psalm 51:1-6

Theodicy

When we look at our lives, it becomes very easy to overlook the countless gifts and grace that God has granted each one of us. Rather many of us find ourselves living day by day focusing on our trials and tribulations as we fall into the trap of asking "why me?" Because of that, we stop focusing on living lives that honor and glorify God, and thus begin living lives that focus on feeling sorry for ourselves.

However, by allowing ourselves to think this way, we become skeptical to the idea of theodicy. In other words, we start to disagree with the thought that God can be both omnipotent and loving yet still allow pain and suffering to exist in the world. If God loves us so dearly, and is truly all-powerful, then why would he allow bad things to happen to us?

Once again it is Satan we find waiting in the wings to plant that seed of doubt in our minds. But by looking closely we find that this is simply one more of the tools he uses to further alienate us from God. Through his deception we begin to fool ourselves into thinking that the pain we are experiencing has been brought forth by our own account. Another way to think of it is the theory that in the eyes of God, every person's suffering is indicative of their own sin. But to think like this is to fall into Satan's trap! It is much too easy for Satan to blindly lead us into believing that the trials we face are simply because of the bad things we've done in the past.

If the skeptics are right, and the idea of theodicy is not true, then what case is to be made for the trials of Job? Here we find a completely upright and righteous servant of God, yet he still faced greater adversity and trials than any of us could begin to fathom for ourselves. His friends and even his wife prompted him to give into the trap of believing that God must be punishing him for all his wrong doings. But Job knew better! He fully understood that God often allows misfortune to find even his greatest of saints.

It's because of this we can begin to realize that we've been asking the wrong question all along! The question for our misfortune can no longer be one of why bad things may happen to bad people. But more so, it becomes a question of why do bad things happen to good people?

In my opinion, God does whatever it takes in order to get our attention. He will go to the ends of the earth and do whatever he feels is necessary to help guarantee our salvation. Our earthly life is not the greatest concern of God. It's our eternal life that he truly cares about, and he will do whatever he sees fit to open our eyes to that truth.

Nowhere are examples of this more prevalent than in all the incidences that fill the pages of the Bible. Remember Shadrach, Meshach, and Abednego? What about Daniel or Lazarus? God not only gained the attention of those individuals, but he gained the attention of the individuals around them. Do you think that people turned a blind eye to three men not burning in the fierce fires of a furnace? What about a man who survived a night trapped in a pit with hungry lions? And who could deny that an entire community did not realize the awesome power of God's hand after watching their dead brother and son be brought back to life after four days in the grave.

God knows how to get our attention! Granted you may not find yourself floating on an ark or parting the Red Sea, but he will find a way to speak to you. Regardless of how quiet or loud it may be, God still works in our lives. It simply becomes our task to be vigilant enough to hear what he's trying to say.

You would think that being swallowed by a whale, and then spat back up in order to put you back on course, would be a fairly eye opening experience. That was almost the case for Jonah. It's with Jonah that we find a man not much different than ourselves. Here we see a man who had the opinion that he knew best. It was his will, not God's that he wanted done. Jonah tried to run from God's plan, but God had a different idea and used an amazing feat to put Jonah back on track. Regardless, Jonah reluctantly failed to open his eyes! He did not see what God wanted for his heart, and because of that he missed the big picture. He not only overlooked God's ultimate plan, but more importantly he failed to see God's compassion.

Don't be a Jonah! Don't miss out on what God is trying to tell you. God doesn't always shout at us as he did in the case of Jonah. Sometimes he simply whispers. God has an important message he wants to share with us. He desires to share his message of salvation, and will do whatever it takes to place that message in our lives. We just need to recognize that he's speaking, and then listen to what it is he has to say.

Job 5:6-11

Looking For Answers

As humans it's a painfully hard fact that we are not without sin. My brother wasn't perfect; I should know since I was by his side for 34 years, and know first hand all the things that we did. With that said, I won't even begin to try and fool anyone into thinking I am without fault myself. Yet before you begin to judge me or anyone else for that matter, you first need to take a close look at yourself. By doing so, you'll realize that you too will not find the title of Saint listed before your name. (Or have you forgotten Romans 3:23?)

So where does that leave us? Plain and simple, it leaves us standing in the shadow of the cross. The greatest story of God is the overwhelming love and grace he has for us. He loved us so deeply that he sent his son to die for us. What an amazing fact! Jesus took on an unimaginable amount of pain and suffering to guarantee the salvation for each one of us; regardless of how undeserving we all may be! Sit back and think about that for a minute. He was beaten, mocked, tortured, nailed to a cross, and then left to die!

What type of unfathomable love would ever possess someone to fulfill such a task? Who are we to receive such undeserved compassion? Simply put we are God's children. Just as a parent has unfathomable and unconditional love for his or her own child, God has the exact same type of love for each one of us!

It's God's love that should be seen as the center for everything that comes to us. His infinite love for us is the root of any answer for every question we may have for him. It's love that creates the basis for the gifts God gives, the forgiveness he grants, the mercy he shows, and the empathy he has for us. Ultimately though it's that unfathomable love that is the nucleus for the salvation he wants us to receive. To better understand this, we need to dig deeper into each of these things that radiate from the core of this unconditional love.

It's always easiest to focus on the bad circumstances in our lives. Maybe you've dealt with a job loss, an illness, or death in your family. The bad things that happen to us have an easy way of fogging our vision. And when that occurs, the Devil is right there to once again tempt us. Emphasizing our misfortunes is just one more tool he uses to temp us so as to create a wide chasm between God, and us. However, it is absolutely critical we overcome his trap of temptation. We must recognize it, and then truly begin to focus on the good. It's when bad things happen that we need to step back for a minute and begin to deeply examine our lives. It's not until we do this, that we will actually begin to see the bounty of gifts God has granted us.

All too often we connect a gift with something that can be purchased. But if that's our only measure of a gift from God, then we have once again failed. Maybe he has granted you a bounty of riches, but that type of wealth is merely a temporary bonus for your life. Are you too quick to forget about your family or friends? What about the talents he has granted you, or the beauty of the world around you? The true gifts he grants us are much larger than a mere dollar bill. And it's not until we can see past the price tag that we will truly begin to understand the connection with love.

"Father, forgive them;" was the prayer of Jesus while he hanged nailed to the cross. Forgive them? He was wrongly accused, tormented, beaten, bloodied, and then hanged on a cross to die for sins that were not his. Yet, in the midst of all his pain he still offers the prayer for God to forgive. When you first look at this picture everything about it seems completely wrong. But it's not until you look at it closer that you see the very essence of what seems wrong is actually what makes everything right.

Jesus was the epitome of forgiveness, and it was Jesus who first showed us how to forgive. In Luke 17:3-4 we find Jesus teaching his disciples about forgiveness. In that verse we find Jesus saying: "Be on your guard! If another disciple sins, you must rebuke the offender, and if there is repentance, you must forgive. And if the same person sins against you seven times a day, and turns back to you seven times and says, 'I repent,' you must forgive." To expand upon this topic we need to look no further than Matthew 18:22 when Peter asked Jesus how many times he should forgive someone. Jesus' responded by saying: "not seven times, but seventy-seven times." In other words, the answer for Peter, and for us is that there is no answer. There is no magic number of when forgiveness should or will stop.

Jesus didn't stop there. He didn't simply just talk about forgiveness. It wasn't just his words that would become the lessons and example for us. By dying on the cross, he himself became the ultimate example of forgiveness. Not only did his death grant us the salvation from our sins, but at no point during his torture did he stop living the words he had taught. "Father, forgive them; for they know not what they are doing."

Mercy can often be confused with forgiveness. And while the two do go nicely together, forgiveness is more often the result of mercy, not it's equal. Mercy is the feeling of compassion or pity you have for an individual. Where forgiveness is the act of pardoning an individual. In other words, because of the mercy you felt toward someone, you have forgiven them of their debt.

One of my favorite parables in the Bible is a perfect example for the subject of mercy. Matthew 18:23-35 reads: "For this reason the kingdom of heaven may be compared to a king who wished to settle accounts with his slaves. When he began the reckoning, one who owed him ten thousand talents was brought to him; and as he could not pay, his lord ordered him to be sold, together with his wife and children and all his possessions, and payment to be made. So the slave fell on his knees before him, saying, 'Have patience with me, and I will pay you everything.' And out of pity for him, the lord of that slave released him and forgave him the debt. But that same slave, as he went out, came upon one of his fellow slaves who owed him a hundred denarii; and seizing him by the throat, he said, 'Pay what you owe.' Then his fellow slave fell down and pleaded with him, 'Have patience with me, I will pay you.' But he refused; then he went and threw him into prison until he would pay the debt. When his fellow slaves saw what had happened, they were greatly distressed, and they went and reported to their lord all that had taken place. Then his lord summoned him and said to him, 'You wicked slave! I forgave you all that debt because you pleaded with me. Should you not have mercy on your fellow slave, as I have had mercy on you? And in anger his lord handed him over to be tortured until he would pay his entire debt. So my heavenly Father will do to every one of you, if you do not forgive your brother or your sister from your heart."

In the exact same way, God forgives because of the undeserving mercy he has for each and every one of us. His mercy is derived from love, and is a perfect example of how he lives by what He teaches. It's a lesson we must not turn a deaf ear toward, for just as God has, he expects us to do in our lives as well.

Empathy is best explained as the intellectual identification with feelings, thoughts, or attitudes of another individual. In other words, you can emotionally place yourself in the situation of what someone else is experiencing. Often times these emotional identifications are direct results of having lived similar experiences yourself. With that said, how then are we to understand the idea of an all-powerful God as having empathy toward us?

I feel the easiest way, is for us to closely read Mark 14:32-36 where it reads: They went to a place called Gethsemane; and he said to his disciples, "Sit here while I pray." He took with him Peter and James and John, and began to be distressed and agitated. And he said to them, "I am deeply grieved, even to death; remain here, and keep awake." And going a little farther, he threw himself on the ground and prayed that, if it were possible, the hour might pass from him. He said, "Abba, Father, for you all things are possible; remove this cup from me; yet, not what I want, but what you want.

What an incredible scene of equality! Here we find the Son of God struggling with and tormented by emotions and feelings we may have experienced in our own lives. It is there among the Olive trees in Gethsemane that we find God intertwined with humanity. Though it seems hard to believe, it is in that garden which we are able to find God as being closest to you and me.

God understands our anguish; He can relate to our despair and our suffering. He can comprehend all our fears, and identifies with our struggles and the ache in our hearts. He does all of this not merely because of his omniscience, but because he has experienced it all for himself! Just look at Luke 22 verse 44 where it reads: In his anguish he prayed more earnestly, and his sweat became like great drops of blood falling down on the ground. Does this sound like a God who cannot empathize with us?

The next time you find yourself drowning in despair or surrounded by your sorrow, read through Mark 14 and realize that you're not alone. God loves you, and he empathizes with your pain. But it's not until you open your eyes that you'll realize just how close God is to you. So go pay a visit to Gethsemane, but be sure to pay close attention. For it's among the twisted branches of the Olive trees that you will find a man who loves you more than you can fathom.

Psalm 63:1-4

Follow The Right Path

Even if you forget everything I have written thus far, my prayer is that these next two chapters will stay close to your heart and linger in your mind. This is not because I feel these two chapters are more meaningful, or that they will bestow some type of amazing revelation to you. No, my main wish is that God will use the information in these next two chapters to reward you the same hope and encouragement that he so gracefully granted to me.

Bad things are going to happen in your life. You will inevitably face trials and eventually find heartache. There will even be moments when you feel there's absolutely no way your life could possibly get any worse than it is at that very moment. Regardless, when you find that the adverse struggles of life have left you broken or crippled; you cannot lose faith! It's imperative that you do not lose sight of the unconditional love that God has for you! But most of all, you cannot forget that the temporary trappings of life are just that; temporary!

When Clinton died, I allowed the painful experience of that moment to fog my vision. Because of my immediate anger I missed out on a simply incredible experience. The moment someone is called home and given the gift of their eternal life in heaven is a truly amazing experience! To be one of the select people standing beside that person as you witness their entry through those pearly gates is an honor that is hard to describe! After all, going to heaven does only happen once in a person's lifetime.

Where we seem to stumble as humans is that we allow our selfishness to overrun the situation. Instead of our love for that person allowing us to be joyful for them. We allow selfishness to create despair and pity for ourselves. It's not until you can break through the fog of the moment that you truly realize you were not focusing on the right person, and because of that you completely missed out on the incredible circumstances of that moment.

Dealing with the loss of a loved one, or any type of trial in our lives for that matter, becomes a very slippery slope. Ultimately the situation that is creating the pain in our life will initially begin to shift our mindset toward a self-centered attitude. And why shouldn't it? After all it's happening to us isn't it? But it's exactly this "self-centered pity party" that I have been warning you about all along! It's that selfish attitude of "me" that we need to overcome and conquer!

By no means am I suggesting that you shouldn't greave or feel sad about your loss. Honestly, I'm not sure if it's even possible not to greave when it comes to losing someone you love. Because of that I fully understand the need for grieving. I also support the thought that there will always be a small piece of you that's afflicted because of how much you miss your loved one. I know this burden completely since I find myself struggling daily with an ongoing sadness from the loss of my brother.

However, regardless of our feelings, we cannot allow that sadness to rule the situation, or our lives for that matter. You cannot overlook the good that can be found in the moment despite how bad it may seem at the time. You cannot lose sight of where our focus needs to be, that focus needs to be on Jesus Christ.

In my opinion, Romans 8:31-39 does an outstanding job of explaining this. In these verses we find Paul granting words of encouragement to the Christians in Rome where he writes: "What then are we to say about these things? If God is for us, who is against us? He who did not withhold his own son, but gave him up for all of us, will he not with him also give us everything else? Who will bring any charge against God's elect? It is God who justifies. Who is to condemn? It is Jesus Christ, who died, yes, who was raised, who is at the right hand of God, who indeed intercedes for us. Who will separate us from the love of Christ? Will hardship, or distress, or persecution, or famine, or nakedness, or peril, or sward? As it is written,

"For your sake we are being killed all
day long; we are accounted as sheep

to be slaughtered."

No, in all these things we are more than conquerors though him who loved us. For I am convinced that neither death, nor life, nor angels, nor rulers, nor things present, nor things to come, nor power, nor height, nor depth, nor anything else in all creation, will be able to separate us from the love of God in Jesus Christ the Lord."

The words Paul wrote in that letter are just as relevant for you and me today, as they were for the Romans in 57 A.D. Regardless of the gigantic leaps in progress and improvements that have spawned dramatic changes over the past 2000 years, there has always been, and will always be pain and suffering in our lives. Paul understood this, and he directs us to see past the pain, and drive toward the purpose. This is his attempt at helping us to focus on what is truly important so that we too can be more than conquerors through Christ.

So where do we go from here? For me, I find myself back in my car as I travel that winding road to work on that early September morning. There I am, back at that pivotal moment when God opened my eyes and revealed just how far down the wrong path I had wondered. Hopefully, you can find yourself there with me as I turn that corner and break the crest of that hill. I pray that you too will see the need to call out to God and ask him to: "Open My Eyes!" After all dummy... It's not about *you*!

John 12:24-26

Final Thoughts

As I stated in the speech I gave at Clint's funeral, I learned an unfathomable amount of information from what he taught me during his short 36 year of life. However, what I didn't realize was that even though his body may be gone, he still is teaching me to this very day. But this time he's not merely teaching me life lessons or ways to be a more "manly man." Instead, what he is teaching me, is one of the most important lessons he ever has taught during his life as an educator. The lesson he's teaching me now is about my walk with God, and about becoming the Christian I need to be by mirroring the type of Christian that he had been.

As I dug deeper into this idea, I began to narrow down and intensely focus on a few of these important lessons I felt were key to a Christ filled life. I would like to end by sharing some of these lessons, as it's my prayer they will touch your heart and open your eyes just as they have for me.

1) Decide each day to forgive.

Just as Jesus forgives each and every one of us, so should we forgive those around us. The statement “I cannot forgive you” is actually a false statement. What you are actually saying when those words leave your lips is the bold statement of: “I choose not to forgive you.” But are we too quick to remember that God’s forgiveness sees no limit in our lives? Who then are we to not forward the same loving forgiveness to everyone else around us? It is essential that we have a decided heart for forgiveness. Because it is then, and only then that we can forgive as Christ first forgave us.

2) *Pray!*

Prayer is an essential part of our walk with God. It’s your personal conversation with your loving Father. Prayer cannot be limited to a mere moment of panic or immediate personal need. Prayer must be approached no differently than conversations you would have with a best friend on earth. You would be hard pressed to keep a friend if you only saw them as good for helping you with problems or listening to your complaints.

With that in mind, you must forward God the same respect by sharing with Him not only the pain, but also the joys in your life. Your prayers should be personal, but cannot be limited to just one person. They should be an unselfish, heartfelt, and thought filled conversation. God doesn’t want to hear a broken record any more than you do.

Most importantly though, it is absolutely essential that you take the time to pray often! Maybe it's just the athlete in me, but in my mind, prayer is no different than a muscle in your body. It will never get any stronger unless you exercise it daily!

3) *Earnestly seek wisdom.*

Wisdom is the cornerstone to many of life's greatest gifts. Wisdom has built kings, granted riches, found comfort, and offered peace. Wisdom is all around you and is constantly yours for the taking. Wisdom can be found in the books you read and the music you listen to. Sometimes you'll find it in a movie you'll watch, or a class that you'll take. Yet two of the greatest places to start seeking wisdom are through reading your Bible, and by talking with your pastor. If you don't have a church, go find one! Just make sure you find one that speaks to your heart, and does not simply fill a denomination.

In addition to all those great options, it's still my opinion one of the best places to seek wisdom is through your family and friends. Surround yourself with them, and talk to them daily! I've done my part by offering you some options, now it's up to you to offer the follow through! This is the point where it becomes your task to seek the wisdom you deserve, and the best way to start is by asking for help. You're not being strong by facing your trials alone; you're simply being stupid. Your friends and family are there to help you, and when you find yourself in need, the insight they can offer is often quite amazing. But most important of all, is your need to seek out the wisdom of God. Since it is he who can be seen as one of your greatest friends and your closest of family members.

It's your father in heaven who can offer the peace you seek when you've come up empty handed here on earth. So remember, the next time the storms of life are blowing in your direction, or the fog of despair has surrounded you in self-pity. Open your eyes and reach out your hand out for help. But pay close attention! Since you may just find that the first hand reaching back, is one that's been pierced by nails.

Proverbs 1:2-9

References

Chapter 3: Why?
Mark Schultz, "Walking Her Home," Broken and Beautiful, Warner Bros. Records Christian Division, World Entertainment (September 2006)

Chapter 6: Not Completely Blind
James 4:14, Holy Bible, The New Revised Standard Version, World Bible Publishers, Inc. 1989

Chapter 7: What Now?
MercyMe, "This Life" The Generous Mr. Lovewell, Simpleville Music, INO Records (May 2010)

Chaper 8: Starting to See
MercyMe, "I can only imagine", Almost There, Simpleville Music, INO Records (August 2001)

Chapter 8 Starting to See
Casting Crowns, "The Alter and the Door", The Alter and the Door, Beach Street Records/ Reunion Records, Sony Music (August 2007)

Copyright © 2007 My Refuge Music (BMI) (adm. at EMICMGPublishing.com) / Club Zoo Music (BMI) / SWECS Music (BMI) All rights reserved. Used by permission.

©2007 Sony/ATV Music Publishing LLC and My Refuge Music. All rights on behalf of Sony/ATV Music Publishing LLC administered by Sony/ATV Music Publishing LLC, 8 Music Square West, Nashville, TN 37203. All rights reserved. Used by permission.

Chapter 9: Eyes Wide Open

Casting Crowns, "The Alter and the Door", The Alter and the Door, Beach Street Records/ Reunion Records, Sony Music (August 2007)

Chapter 10: 20/20 Vision

Isaiah 57:1-2, Holy Bible, The New Revised Standard Version, World Bible Publishers, Inc. 1989

Chapter 10: 20/20 Vision

Mark 9:24, Holy Bible, The New Revised Standard Version, World Bible Publishers, Inc. 1989

Chapter 10: 20/20 Vision

Matthew 26:53-54, Holy Bible, The New Revised Standard Version, World Bible Publishers, Inc. 1989

Chapter 12: Looking for Answers
Luke 17:3-4, Holy Bible, The New Revised Standard Version, World Bible Publishers, Inc. 1989

Chapter 12: Looking for Answers
Matthew 18:22-35, Holy Bible, The New Revised Standard Version, World Bible Publishers, Inc. 1989

Chapter 12: Looking for Answers
Mark 14:32-36, Holy Bible, The New Revised Standard Version, World Bible Publishers, Inc. 1989

Chapter 12: Looking for Answers
Mark 14:32-36, Holy Bible, The New Revised Standard Version, World Bible Publishers, Inc. 1989

Chapter 12: Looking for Answers
Luke 22:44, Holy Bible, The New Revised Standard Version, World Bible Publishers, Inc. 1989

Chapter 13: Follow the Right Path
Romans 8:31-39, Holy Bible, The New Revised Standard Version, World Bible Publishers, Inc. 1989

CPSIA information can be obtained at www.ICGtesting.com
Printed in the USA
LVOW050403300612

288269LV00001B/54/P

9 781456 041939